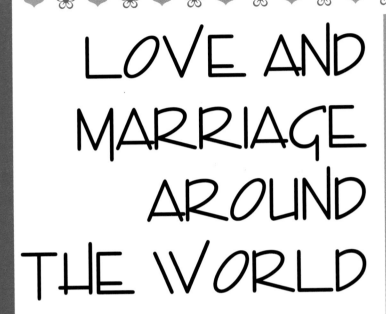

LOVE AND MARRIAGE AROUND THE WORLD

CAROL GELBER

The Millbrook Press
Brookfield, Connecticut

Published by The Millbrook Press, Inc.,
2 Old New Milford Road
Brookfield, CT 06804

Photographs courtesy of New York Public Library Picture Collection:
p. 8; © Donna DeCesare/Impact Visuals: p. 13; Gamma Liaison:
pp. 16-17 (© Kaku Kurita), 62 (© Renato Rotolo), 64-65 (© Sailler-
Airone); National Geographic Image Collection: pp. 24-25 (© James
P. Blair), 40-41 (© Sam Abell), 45 (© Otis Imboden); Anthro Photo:
pp. 34-35 (© Richard Katz), 50-51 (© Lila Abu-Lughod); Turkish
Tourist Office (Franz Edson): p. 54; Barbara Beckerman: p. 72

Library of Congress Cataloging-in-Publication Data
Gelber, Carol.
Love and marriage around the world / Carol Gelber.
p.   cm.
Includes index.
Summary: Discusses customs around the world relating to the
taboos and societal conventions surrounding love and marriage.
ISBN 0-7613-0102-X (lib. bdg.)
1. Marriage customs and rites—Juvenile literature. [1. Marriage
customs and rites. 2. Weddings.] I. Title.
NRR GT2600.G45 1998
392.5—dc2l   97-1695
CIP   AC

Contents

CHAPTER 1

The Roots of Marriage

How many ways are there to get married? The answer, of course, is that there are as many traditional ways as there are societies—and some new ways, too. The shape that marriage customs take depends not only on the bride and groom but also on their families and their community. Who can marry? Who cannot? What is a proper wedding? Every culture answers these questions with its own set of rules, rituals, and expectations. Our history, religious beliefs, and the way we make a living all influence how—and whom—we marry.

But why do we marry at all? To answer this question we must look back many thousands of years to early members of our own species. Nowadays we think of marriage as

"With this ring I thee wed," says an American groom.

Today, daughter, you meet the boy we have chosen for you," announces an Indian father.

"I bring you cattle for your daughter," says a Zulu suitor.

You must not marry into the Coyote Clan," warns a Hopi mother.

the first step toward starting a new family. Yet long before the earliest marriage ceremony the family came first. The need to share food and to care for children are some of the important considerations that made the family the building block of society.

Keep in mind that humans belong to the same animal group—primates—as apes and monkeys. Like these other species, we have a long history of adapting to changes in our environment. Comparing ourselves to species similar to our own can help us understand our own behavior.

Studies of other primates, for example, tell us something about the development of human family life. For one thing, they show that group life provides protection for the young. Young apes and monkeys are dependent on adults for a very long time. Tiny, helpless human infants make extra-heavy demands on their parents. A human baby must be carried, while a baby monkey is able to cling to its mother as she swings through the treetops. A chimpanzee reaches adulthood at nine years, but a child of that age still needs a caretaker. In fact, it takes fourteen to twenty years for humans to reach full physical maturity, much longer than any other animal.

The earliest members of our species lived in small hunting bands of related families. Survival depended on belonging to a group that shared food and the care of children. Women with babies or small children in tow couldn't go hunting. They stayed close to a safe shelter as they gathered plant foods such as edible roots, nuts, and fruits. Men roved together far and wide to hunt and to defend their territory. If they returned empty-handed, the group survived on plant foods gathered by the women. Everyone benefited by sharing. Furthermore, a child whose mother and father cooperated had the best chance of growing up. No cartoon "caveman" who dragged his woman around by the hair could expect to leave many descendants!

Anthropologists reconstruct the life of early humans by studying other primates, by digging up the past as archaeologists, and by studying the few remaining modern-day peoples who live in hunting bands. These studies suggest that our ancestors made alliances with other groups by exchanging women. They understood, just as we do, that seizing food or mates makes enemies, while exchanging food and mates creates allies.

If women left the group they were born into to become the wives and mothers of their neighbors, both groups would widen their territory and their circle of kinfolk. When food was scarce or hostile strangers appeared, each group could count on help from the other.

We could say that marriage came into being when groups of hunter-gatherers agreed to exchange women. Perhaps a man took a neighbor's sister as a wife and sent his neighbor one of his own sisters in exchange.

In this romantic view of prehistoric life it appears that a trade is about to take place—a bear for a wife.

A similar system was practiced by the Mbuti pygmies of Central Africa when the anthropologist Colin Turnbull lived among them in the 1950s. A Mbuti man who wished to marry had to provide a wife for a member of his bride's family. The Mbuti said this was necessary to ensure that neither of their groups was left without women. One Mbuti man's sister who was reluctant to be "exchanged" infuriated her newly married brother. Why, he demanded, did she refuse to marry when she was as strong as an ox? She was too lazy to get married, her brother complained. He and her mother tormented the girl until she agreed to marry one of her new sister-in-law's brothers. If she didn't, her brother's new wife would have to return to her own family.

Only some 11,000 years ago, the entire population of the world lived like the Mbuti in small hunting and gathering bands. All humans foraged for their food, made their own tools, and had few personal possessions. Then, with the development of agriculture about 10,000 years ago, human society gradually changed. As people learned to cultivate grains and domesticate animals, they began to settle into permanent villages.

There was an explosion of new lifestyles as hunters became farmers and herders, villages became towns, and towns grew into cities. A person might be a king or a slave, a farmer or a weaver, a soldier or a scholar. Now that it was possible to own more and more things, marriage concerned itself with property and social importance: houses, land, animals, jobs, and titles. Many new questions were raised. Did marriage involve property rights? Who was a legitimate heir? A wealthy man could support more than one wife. Why not two? Why not twenty?

Gradually people decided upon the answers to these questions. Certain ideas were universal, however. Marriage was a public alliance between families. Its purpose was to create a permanent bond between a man and a woman that would produce and protect the next generation. It spelled out the rights and obligations of a couple and established their legitimate descendants.

To this day these basic principles are the foundation of marriage systems around the world.

CHAPTER 2

Close—But Not Too Close

This old English counting rhyme is supposed to tell a girl who her future husband will be, and she hopes the count lands on an exciting prospect. But whatever the prediction, she will probably marry someone very much like herself. For if a rich man sometimes marries a penniless beauty or a king weds a commoner, these matches are exceptions. Most people marry someone who shares their social position, wealth, religion, and race.

In fact, most marriages everywhere are made within a narrow group of people with similar backgrounds who are not too closely related. People have long realized that it is important for the health and strength of the group not to marry a close blood relative.

Rich man, poor man,

Beggarman, thief,

Doctor, lawyer,

Merchant, chief.

Most societies have rules that forbid marriage between close kin, usually up to cousins of some degree.

There are, however, places where a cousin is the preferred spouse. One such place is the Middle East. In Egypt marriage to a cousin is the ideal for many village people. Parents hope to marry their daughter to her father's brother's son. In Oman, a tiny country on the Arabian Sea, until 1971 a man had a legal right to marry his cousin even if her father objected to the match.

"Trade out, marry in" is a folk saying in Iran where marriage between cousins is seen as creating lasting unions and strengthening family connections. Sometimes that old belief turns modern young people against marriage to cousins—they want to be independent and free from their family's interference. Furthermore, young men say that a stranger makes a gentle, obedient wife, while a cousin feels free to nag and complain.

Marriage between the very closest of relatives—brother and sister—is not unheard of. Egyptian pharaohs sometimes married their sisters, as did Hawaiian royalty and the Inca rulers in pre-Columbian South America. This marriage system kept power and wealth inside a small family circle. And since these ruling families claimed to be descended

Everybody in town comes out to witness and celebrate a wedding in a small town outside Cairo, Egypt.

from the gods, brother-sister marriage also kept their sacred bloodlines "pure."

For centuries the royal families of Europe also intermarried to consolidate their political power. Blue-blooded cousins were married to each other so frequently that by the early twentieth century all of European royalty was related. The present queen of England, Elizabeth II, and her husband, the Duke of Edinburgh, are third cousins, for example.

Although most of us don't marry for political purposes, we usually do want a mate who is acceptable to our own family or group. In some cases that means following strict rules of *endogamy,* or marrying only people from our own ethnic group, social class, or religion. This kind of marriage pattern keeps a group together.

Sometimes the acceptable limits are people from the same village. This is the case in rural Turkey and in some Maya Indian communities in Mexico and Central America. In one Mayan village in Mexico, marriage with outsiders or with someone with the same last name is frowned on, but first cousins are free to marry. In the Andes Mountains of Peru, Quechua-speaking Indians also prefer to marry within their own small communities. Since these Andean villagers ban marriages between first or second cousins, finding an eligible mate can be a very difficult business.

Religious groups may promote marriages among their members or even ban marriage to outsiders. Members of the

Unification Church, for instance, are not allowed to marry outside their religious family. Church leaders select the partners. Members believe that the chosen mate was predestined for them. These brides and grooms may never meet until their wedding day. Sometimes they are married in a mass ceremony like the one held in 1995 in the Olympic Stadium in Seoul, South Korea. The world's largest wedding ever, it united more than 35,000 Unification Church couples from all over the world.

Orthodox Jews also ban interreligious marriages. Mormons reserve a special wedding ceremony "for all time and eternity" for members only. In the past Catholics had to get special permission from Rome to marry a non-Catholic. Today it is easier for them to marry someone of another faith, but they must promise to raise their children as Catholics. In the Islamic world it is assumed that children will follow their father's religion, so a Muslim man is free to marry a woman of another religion. A woman, however, may not marry a non-Muslim.

In India marriage within one's own caste is the rule. Since ancient times, Indian society has been divided into hundreds of castes and subcastes, which once corresponded to inherited occupations. Brahmans, who were traditionally priests, rank at the top. At the bottom of the scale are the people who for centuries have done work that was considered dirty and degrading.

In this rigidly ranked society, marriage outside of one's caste is not tolerated. A village boy may know of a girl he would like to marry. She may come from a respectable family, be a hard worker, and be well liked by the boy's own family. But if the village priest decrees that her caste is unacceptable, the marriage will not take place. A mixed-caste marriage would bring disgrace on both families and ruin the chances of brothers and sisters to marry well. There are even reports of village mobs murdering mixed-caste couples.

Endogamy can be enforced by legal means or by cultural rules. In the United States intermarriage has integrated many European immigrants from different ethnic groups. But the melting pot of American life has produced relatively few interracial marriages. One of the reasons is that until fairly recently the United States has had laws against interracial marriage. Americans be-

This picture shows some of the 20,000 brides and grooms who were married in a 1992 mass ceremony in Seoul's Olympic Stadium.

gan to outlaw such marriages in the late seventeenth century. As recently as the 1930s marriage between partners of different races was against the law in more than half the states. It was only in 1967 that the Supreme Court declared such laws unconstitutional.

Sometimes society calls for a marriage pattern that is the opposite of endogamy. *Exogamy* requires a person to marry outside his or her particular group. Marriage between very close relatives, for example, is taboo in *every* modern-day society. But just who is too close? People answer that question differently. Sometimes people who are forbidden to marry are not close kin at all, but clan brothers and sisters. Clans are large groups of people who claim to be descended from the same ancestor, often a mythical superhero or supernatural animal. Marriage between clan members is forbidden, even if the group includes thousands of people. In some places it was believed that marriage between clan members was likely to call down the wrath of the gods. The Navajo in the American Southwest thought that people who married into their own clan were either crazy or practicing witchcraft.

Then there are cultures in which both exogamy and endogamy are practiced. On the northwest coast of Alaska the Tlingit people belong to clans. A boy belonging to the Raven clan may be encouraged to marry a girl from the Wolf clan (exogamy), but he may also be expected to marry a girl with his same religious background (endogamy). In fact, most cultures are both exogamous and endogamous, but they draw the boundaries at different places.

For the Apache in Arizona, clan membership was so complicated that a girl in search of a husband had to rely on elderly relatives to determine who was eligible. Even talking to a clan member of the opposite sex was frowned on. Girls were told, "Don't flirt with your clan relatives, because it's not right. That way you will become poor and won't be able to make a good marriage."

In the 1930s the anthropologist Ruth Underhill worked among Indians in the American Southwest. She found that teachers at a school for Indian teenagers were unhappy because every party they gave for the students was a complete flop. Boys stayed on one side of the room and girls on the other. Sometimes they kept their backs turned to each other. "Indians are so unsociable," one young teacher complained. Then Underhill discovered that the students were clan brothers and sisters. For them, mixing at a party was a shocking, shameful idea.

On the other side of the world, in 1997, South Korea declared as unconstitutional a centuries-old ban on marriages between same-clan couples—people with the same family name and ancestral village. Until then, even couples who shared only the same last name faced public disapproval if they married. To complicate matters, millions of Koreans have the same last names—22 percent of South Korean families are named Kim, for example.

One South Korean university student said, "When I'm introduced to someone, I very casually ask what her name is, and if I find out that it's the same as mine, it puts a mark against her right there." Many young people felt obliged to give up their true love for someone with a different last name. Sometimes a same-clan couple lived together without getting married. They hoped to marry in the future, since about every ten years the government lifted the ban for one year. Fourteen thousand marriages were registered when the ban was lifted in 1988. Now that same clan marriages are legal, about 60,000 couples already living together in 1997 will be free to marry.

Every society has its own traditions and rules for choosing the best marriage partner. In general, the rules make it clear that families prefer their members to marry people just like themselves.

CHAPTER 3

Making the Match

So says the old jump-rope rhyme. But in many places love is not in the picture at all. Through most of human history, in fact, courtship and romantic love had little to do with selecting a mate.

At one time parents everywhere chose their children's spouses. They believed it was too risky to leave such important decisions in the hands of the young, and it was too easy for a girl or boy to fall in love with the wrong person. An unsuitable match might threaten the bonds of kinship and the family's reputation and property. Marriage was a duty owed to one's family. It was safest to let wise, experienced parents use their heads and not their hearts to arrange such important matters.

First comes love,

Then comes marriage,

Then comes the bride

With a baby carriage . . .

Even today arranged marriages are customary in large parts of the world, especially where girls are segregated and kept at home after they reach marriageable age. This is the case in much of the Middle East. In Saudi Arabia, for example, a young man depends on his female relatives for information about possible brides. Marriage negotiations begin with a visit of the young man's womenfolk to a potential bride's house to "take the pulse" of her mother. The visitors don't reveal that they are interested in the girl, but they try to find out if she has been promised to someone else, or if she wants to finish school before marriage. If the girl is suitable, her father will get a marriage proposal from the groom's family.

In the past a Saudi girl wasn't told that she was getting married until just before the wedding. Once she found out she might be given a photograph of her husband-to-be or catch a glimpse of him from behind closed shutters. The bride and groom met for the first time on their wedding day. Today, although no dating is allowed, couples meet briefly at the girl's home. A modern girl may even discuss with her parents a suitor's personal qualities. But she won't talk about love. To be in love before marriage suggests that a couple are sweethearts who place physical attraction before a partner's character.

In Egypt it is common for a young man to ask a female relative to find him a suitable bride. At one time in southern Egypt, his mother would visit a girl's home to test her suitability as a daughter-in-law. The girl was supposed to serve his mother a hard-boiled egg, peeled without blemishes, to demonstrate her cooking skills. As she kissed the girl good-bye, the young man's mother would pull on the girl's hair to make sure it was thick and healthy and pinch her bottom to make sure she wasn't frail or bony.

A girl in Turkey is also expected to wait on a suitor's parents when they come to call on her family. It gives her family a chance to show off her abilities and her suitor's family an opportunity to look her over. In Turkish villages men and women do not mingle on social occasions. The bride and groom's mothers stay in the kitchen while their fathers negotiate the marriage arrangements in the living room. The bride-to-be scurries between both groups, serving fruits and nuts and cups of sweet black coffee that she has prepared.

Although China banned arranged marriages in 1950, they are still common in the Chinese countryside. For rural people the traditional purposes of an arranged marriage are still important. Parents are eager to continue the family's male line and family name, to get more help with farmwork, and to have children to support them in old age. Young people are still dependent on their parents for jobs and have little chance to meet members of the opposite sex.

Traditionally, Chinese parents choose their children's partners with the help of a matchmaker. This go-between is called a Hong Niang, after a quick-witted maid servant in an ancient play who helped a poor scholar win the hand of a rich man's daughter. A Hong Niang investigates prospective mates and negotiates the marriage agreement. The matchmaker is careful to pair partners of equal status, to "match wooden doors to wooden doors and bamboo doors to bamboo doors." Costly gifts are involved, and neither family wants to lose face.

Until about fifty years ago, poor Chinese families often sold daughters to other families to raise as future daughters-in-law. These "little brides" saved their own family the expense of raising them and saved their adopted family the cost of a traditional marriage. Young people found this kind of marriage especially disagreeable. Adopted daughters-in-law were often mistreated. A

A procession of a bride and nine of her friends in China. They are traveling to a nearby village where the groom awaits. The men leading the procession are carrying part of the bride's dowry— wine, cake, and shoes she has made for the family of her future husband.

little girl in tears might hear, "Look at her, crying like an adopted daughter!" And if the family prospered, a "little bride" reminded them of how poor they once were.

In China's big cities today, parents no longer choose their children's spouses, but they still have a lot of influence over the choices. Children usually live with their families, and parents try to see that they meet the "right" people. If a Hong Niang is involved, it is apt to be a government-run marriage agency, a singles' club, a newspaper ad—or even a popular TV program called *We Meet Tonight*.

In India arranged marriages are still very much the rule. Finding a husband for his daughter is a father's sacred duty. But "Mr. Right" may be hard to find. First of all, he must be of the same caste and social status. After that, a father must consider the young man's other qualifications. How much does he earn? How much will he inherit? How much dowry (gifts from the bride's family) will his father demand? Finally, is the young man's horoscope well matched with that of the bride-to-be?

The search for a groom begins with both parents consulting friends and relatives and, perhaps, the matrimonial ads in newspapers. A typical ad lists the would-be bride's or groom's caste, age, education, occupation, and salary. No matter what their age, marriage prospects are called "boys" and "girls." A "top boy" is a college graduate with a good job—perhaps as a teacher, lawyer, or doctor.

When a likely prospect is found, the daughter's horoscope is sent to the prospective groom's family. If they are interested in the girl, they send back their son's horoscope. If the horoscopes are a good fit, the dowry negotiations begin.

For a girl to speak up or even to appear interested in her marriage arrangements is considered shameful. She should think of these negotiations as her parents' business. Showing any preference is improper. Parents have even been known to boast that when it came to choosing a husband, their daughter was such a good girl that she had no mind of her own!

Of course, caring parents make every effort to find their child a suitable mate. Their daughter will live with her husband's family, so they will try to find out all they can about his household. Will their daughter be well provided for? Are the brides in that house happy or overworked? How does the mother-in-law treat her other sons' wives?

In some progressive families, the girl and boy are "shown" to each other before the negotiations have gone too far, and if they dislike each other the search begins again. Still, traditionalists insist that it is not a proper arranged marriage if the bride and groom meet before the wedding day. It is, they argue, a modern arranged marriage.

In Japan the way people choose spouses has changed dramatically in recent years. Once all marriages were arranged by parents with the help of a matchmaker. Today it is one in four, and the number is declining. More and more young people are finding their own mates at their colleges or at their jobs. Nevertheless, many Japanese consider arranged marriages to have the best chance of lifelong success. Such marriages, they say, start out cold and grow hot, while love marriages start out hot and grow cold.

Unlike the custom in India, where parents exclude the young people, an arranged marriage in Japan begins with a formal meeting of the prospective bride and groom and their families. Often this meeting takes place in a restaurant or hotel lobby where the couple have a chance to talk to each other. Their families exchange documents concerning their health, education, and ancestry. These documents are studied with care. City people may even hire detectives to investigate a prospect's family. Country people visit the other family's village and ask shopkeepers and neighbors about them. If there are skeletons in the family closet, they had better be closely guarded.

Nowadays the couple may date a few times. It is said that they will be looking for the three "highs": high education, high income, and physical height. If they seem to like each other, they soon will be pressured to marry. All who are involved in the arrangement hope that the couple who came together as strangers will fall in love. If they are too picky, the matchmaker may not want to arrange further introductions.

Marriage in Africa has always been concerned with strengthening family ties and consolidating family property. Customarily, parents or guardians arrange marriages, often between cousins. The Wolof people of Senegal say they prefer to marry a cousin, because cousins are likely to try hard to get along. They won't want to stir up family trouble. And if they do quarrel, the whole family will work to try to smooth things over.

Many an African girl is married to a man to whom she was promised by her family when she was a toddler. In general, girls are dependent on others to arrange their marriages as sometimes women are completely segregated, with little chance to meet potential mates.

In traditional African societies, girls are married when they are very young to much older husbands. Hausa girls in northern Nigeria, for example, are married at twelve or thirteen. Men marry later because they must be able to support a wife. And while an Indian bride's family must provide a dowry, men in some African societies will have to make a large payment (called bridewealth) to the bride's family. In the Democratic Republic of Congo (formerly Zaire), an Azande girl who balks at marrying her father's choice faces social disapproval or even punishment because she is depriving her family of bridewealth.

Making a match is a long and complicated process among the Maya Indians in the Central American country of Guatemala. It begins with a series of visits called "the open door." A young man tells his parents about a girl he would like to marry. His parents ask their village leader to accompany them and their son to the girl's home. They go before daybreak, kneel in front of her doorway, and humbly plead with her parents to open the door. It remains closed. No self-respecting family opens the door on a suitor's first visit. On a second visit the young man's parents bring small gifts of food or liquor. If the girl's parents accept the gifts, the door to marriage has begun to open. If the match is acceptable, they will open the door on the third or fourth visit and offer the young man's parents a drink. He, however, remains on his knees to show respect to his future in-laws.

In Europe and America, and increasingly in other industrialized societies, people find their own mates, often at school or at work. Sometimes single people seek the help of a computerized dating service, or find a mate through the personal ads in the newspapers. However they meet, they hope that love will lead to marriage with a partner who will be a lifelong best friend and companion.

Nonetheless, in large parts of the world marriages arranged by the family remain the customary, respectable way to wed. In either case, both children and parents hope their choices meet with approval.

CHAPTER 4

Fair Exchange

A shower of gifts—from TV sets to toasters and towels—descends on American newlyweds. Gifts begin arriving long before the wedding day, at parties for the bride-to-be and from friends and relatives invited to the ceremony. Both sets of parents will probably give the couple an especially nice wedding gift. Chances are it will be money or something to help them furnish their new home.

Very likely, many of the gifts will be chosen from the couple's wish list at a department store's bridal registry. This computerized list can include anything from a salad bowl to a lawn mower. It helps ensure that the bride and groom get gifts they really want—not Aunt Mary's hand-painted pottery cat and three sets of wind chimes. Sometimes the wedding gifts will be displayed at the bride's home. Friends are invited to "ooh" and "aah" over an array of shiny silver candlesticks and crystal goblets.

Displaying wedding gifts at the bride's home is also a custom in Japan. Gifts from the groom's family are laid out on low wooden tables for guests to admire. The gifts will include traditional items such as a long obi (a kimono sash) to symbolize a long marriage, and a pair of fans to signify that the marriage should open out and expand. The bride's engagement ring may also be on exhibit on its own decorated table.

Why do gifts and weddings seem to go together everywhere? One reason is that friends and relatives want to help a couple get started in their new life. Another is that an exchange of gifts helps cement the relationship between the families of the bride and groom. In some places gifts are meant to compensate a family for the loss of a working member of the household. And sometimes (perhaps more often than people like to admit) families use marriage gifts as a way to show off their wealth and importance.

In most cultures, wedding gifts tend to flow in one direction. Most often, gifts move from the groom's family to the family of the bride. This is a traditional pattern in many places in Africa where the boy's family presents the girl's family with bridewealth. The exact amount is arrived at after long negotiations between the families and with the exchange of other gifts between them. The bride's mother, for example, may receive gifts of food and household items to thank her for the work of raising a daughter.

In African cattle-raising societies—such as the Zulu of South Africa—bridewealth has customarily been a gift of cattle. A girl's family looks at the cattle as compensation for the loss of their child. After all, she will live and work with her husband's family, and her children will be members of his household. The bride's brother will use some of the animals to get his own wife. He is lucky to have a sister. Without her bridewealth he might not be able to accumulate enough cattle to get married.

In Africa today wage labor is replacing farming and cattle raising as a livelihood. Increasingly, cash, not cattle, is demanded as bridewealth. Still, the amount often is so high that a man must wait years to marry and even then have to pay in installments. A Zulu man had this in mind when he said, "We get our wives with difficulty." His wife, on the other hand, would be proud of the large amount he must pay. It shows how much she and her family are valued.

Bridewealth also acts as a kind of marriage insurance. It must be returned if the marriage fails. The difficulties resulting from a failed marriage keep both families interested in making it successful. They will work hard to smooth over quarrels and settle disputes between husband and wife.

Large amounts of cash and gifts for the bride are also customary in the Muslim world of the Middle East. Islamic law calls for the groom to give his bride a gift called the *mahr*, which includes money or some kind of property. Part of the amount is usually held back, to be paid if the couple divorce or the husband dies. In Saudi Arabia the amount due at marriage is at least enough to buy the bride's clothing for a year and to furnish her new home. Prosperous newlyweds receive lavish gifts from both sets of parents: elegant furnishings for their new home along with a luxurious car, for example.

A few years ago the mahr demanded in Saudi Arabia was so high that many men couldn't afford to pay and married girls from Egypt and Lebanon. Soon there were too many Saudi girls without husbands. The government had to make new rules that made it harder to marry a foreigner. There was even talk about lending men money to marry Saudi girls. In the neighboring country of

This large pile of yams is part of the bride's dowry in Fiji.

Oman, the ruling Sultan banned large mahr payments when his soldiers complained that they could not afford to get married. A bride's father who demanded more than a modest, set amount could be called before a judge on serious charges.

In China large gifts from the groom's family are also traditional, especially in the countryside. The Chinese government called this practice "marriage by purchase" and outlawed it in 1950. Still, the custom proved impossible to stamp out in rural areas. Even today the bride's family expects gifts of cash, clothes, and food as well as the cakes sent to announce the marriage. Although both families hold feasts to celebrate the marriage, the groom's family will host the largest and most costly banquet on the wedding day itself. In some places the bride will be expected to pour tea and accept gifts of "lucky money" in red envelopes from the guests.

A Chinese bride brings her own family's gifts, or dowry, to her marriage. Traditionally, her dowry included furniture and bedding and was carried in open carts behind the sedan chair that conveyed her to her husband's household. If her family was very wealthy, her dowry might outdo the groom's gifts. In any case, it was a public display of the status of both families. It showed how much her family could afford—and how much dowry the groom's family could demand.

In recent years many people in China have prospered. Today, some couples are having large, extravagant weddings and are requesting more gifts from their parents. In the 1960s they asked for watches, bikes, and sewing machines. Nowadays they want gold jewelry and expensive appliances such as double-door refrigerators.

In a few large societies in Europe and Asia, a substantial dowry was—and sometimes still is—required of the bride. In eighteenth-century France it was virtually impossible for a girl without a dowry to find a husband. Only a short time ago, most German brides brought a dowry to their marriage. Even today a woman's dowry plays an important role in marriage negotiations among Europe's upper classes.

In India the groom's family may demand an exorbitant amount of dowry. (They may even specify the exact brand of sewing machine or motor scooter they want included.) The bride's family tries to negotiate an amount they can afford—paid in installments. Even so, the cost of the dowry may equal the family's income for two or three years. The Indian author Ved Mehta says that his grandfather told a daughter's suitor:

> She will have plenty of changes of clothes. For winter, for summer, and for monsoon. Day wear and evening wear. There are, of course, the usual ornaments of 22-carat gold. In addition I plan to give you 2,000 rupees. I would like to give you more, but I have four daughters.

It is no wonder that having many daughters is a dreaded burden for a family. Still, a girl who is pretty and well educated will give her parents bargaining power in dowry negotiations. If the bride is a doctor or a lawyer with a large salary, her parents will be able to drive a hard bargain. Her earning power is as good as dowry gold.

Everywhere we look, wedding gifts—whether part of a calculated negotiation or freely given—play an important role in wedding festivities. They help to establish a brand-new family and add pleasure and excitement to the celebration of marriage.

CHAPTER 5

The Big Day

Everybody loves a wedding. Whether it takes place in a magnificent cathedral or in a country meadow, it is always a joyous celebration. Music and flowers, delicious things to eat and drink, and a bride who looks as if she stepped out of a fairy tale add to the gaiety of the occasion. A festive wedding is an auspicious way to begin married life. It launches the newlyweds in a shower of rice, congratulations, and hopes that they will live happily ever after.

Almost every society acknowledges a person's passage into a new stage in life with some kind of ceremony. A baby's christening, a bar (or bat) mitzvah, and a wedding are all examples of these celebrated milestones. Marriage, certainly, is one of the most

Something old,

Something new,

Something borrowed,

Something blue.

important events in anyone's life. It not only makes a person part of a new family, but in many places it is considered the beginning of full adulthood.

Like all rituals, the wedding ceremony is ringed with tradition and superstition. Often the conditions or beliefs that underlie marriage customs are long forgotten. Many old traditions persist because people find drama and meaning in customs that connect them to the past. Traditional good-luck charms— like the ones listed in the verse at the beginning of this chapter—are still worn by many American brides on their wedding day. The bride's veil, her being given away, the wedding flowers, and the rice showered on the newlyweds are other old practices found in wedding ceremonies today.

Veiling the bride is a widespread, ancient practice. One purpose of the veil was to pro-

According to custom, this Japanese bride wears an oversized hat to cover the horns of jealousy, and a small knife at her bosom for ritual suicide in case she should ever dishonor her husband.

tect her from the evil spirits thought to lurk about on ritual occasions. The veil was also a sign of the bride's submission to her husband—the only man with the right to gaze on her beauty. Some Chinese brides went to their weddings not only veiled but entirely concealed in closed sedan chairs. In India today a Muslim bride may remain draped from head to toe throughout the wedding ceremony. On the next day her husband's relatives come to see her face. The bride sits silently with her eyes closed as her veil is briefly lifted. Many months pass before she uncovers her face in the presence of her male in-laws.

The bride's father giving her away at the altar is a reminder that in times past a father had the right to give his daughter in matrimony to whomever he pleased. In fact, our word "wedding" comes from the *weds* (the promises and payments) that a groom in medieval England gave the bride's father in return for her hand.

Flowers, fruits, and cereal grains are symbols of fertility often used in marriage ceremonies. The bride's bouquet, the strewing of flower petals, the rosebud tucked in the groom's lapel, and the shower of rice tell us that the hope for children is an important part of marriage. In France newlyweds were showered with wheat. In Greece the scattering of pomegranate seeds was supposed to ensure fertility. In Scotland breaking an oatcake over the bride's head once had the same meaning.

Like wedding gifts, the wedding itself is likely to be an occasion for showing off a family's economic and social importance. Americans spend millions of dollars a year on bridal gowns fit for princesses, towering wedding cakes, catered banquets, musicians, and—nowadays—on video photographers to record the entire extravaganza.

In Turkey a wedding in the village calls for a whole week of feasting and dancing. Everyone is invited, although men and women's festivities are segregated. Food tables are lined up in front of the bride's house. Nearby, hired musicians play for the village men to dance. Inside the house the bride dances with her girlfriends. Her hands are covered in designs dyed with henna. As new female guests arrive, the bride kisses their hands, then touches them to her forehead as a sign of respect. The women have come to look at her dowry display of scarfs, dresses, towels, and bed linens.

On the day she leaves home, the bride wears a silk pajamalike outfit, embroidered with silver thread. She has a special hairdo of braids interwoven with black yarn and silver tinsel so that they reach her feet. A blue bead is attached to one of the braids to ward off the evil eye.

Leaving home is a sad but exciting moment. Her mother drapes the bride in a sheet and leads her outside. There, completely covered, she is put on a horse and led toward the groom's house by her father. The groom's male relatives gather on the roof of his house to await her arrival. Each one has brought his hunting rifle. When they spot the bride approaching, they fire their guns in the air to welcome her to her new home. The groom lifts her off the horse and takes her inside. A room has been prepared for the bride and groom and decorated with their beautiful wedding gifts. Forty days later the bride's wedding braids are cut off. She is now a married woman.

In China a few decades ago, a new government began a campaign to replace expensive traditional weddings with frugal mass ceremonies. Politically correct "tea and speeches" weddings in public buildings were promoted. In recent years as many Chinese citizens have grown prosperous, the lavish wedding has made a comeback. Many of the ten million or more weddings each year are now the business of wedding agencies. They handle everything from sending the invitations to providing a limousine to drive the bride to the ceremony in a rented hall.

Perhaps nothing, however, matches the splendor of an upper-class wedding in India. It may involve thousands of guests and last for days of feasting and entertainment. One wedding in 1995 featured invitations inscribed on silver platters, a lunch for 12,000 guests, truckloads of flowers, and whole regiments of men on horses.

*The bride's hennaed hands and the
tinsel headdresses of both bride and groom
are long-standing traditions in India.*

Even an average Indian family saves for years to marry a daughter properly. A professional dresser decorates the bride's hands and face with elegant designs. She drapes her in a red sari and all the dowry gold her father can afford: gold bangles up to her elbows, rings on her fingers and toes, a jeweled nose ring, and many pairs of earrings. The splendidly dressed groom customarily arrives for the ceremony riding a white horse, accompanied by musicians and drummers. The wedding rites last for hours, with prayers and chanting by a Hindu priest. At the climax of the ceremony, the groom leads the bride around a sacred fire, each step ensuring a different blessing on their marriage.

Of course, not all marriages everywhere begin with an extravagant wedding. In some places it is hard to say exactly when a couple are married because their transition to the married state is gradual. This is a common pattern in Africa. Among the Shona people of Zimbabwe a church wedding— if there is one—is just an extra ritual in a long process. No marriage is final until the groom has paid his bride's family all of the agreed-upon bridewealth. Since payments are made over a long period, the couple may have children before the payments are completed. In Niger a Fulani woman is regarded as fully married only after she has her first child and her family exchanges gifts with her husband's family.

Many Indians in the Andes Mountains of South America also get married in a lengthy series of steps. A proper relationship begins with negotiations between both sets of parents. Customarily, the couple then live together in a trial marriage for a year or longer. Before the final ceremonies take place, both bride and groom choose godparents who act as marriage counselors and help pay for the wedding festivities.

Andean villages are small, isolated places. Getting legally married is an expensive business, requiring a trip to a town with government offices and a church. In the past village godparents would round up unmarried couples in the spring and arrange a mass marriage ceremony. Even today many church ceremonies include several brides and grooms.

A church wedding in Bolivia involves an exchange of old coins and wedding rings between the bride and groom. To symbolize their union, the priest places silver chains over the couple's heads as they slip on their wedding rings. Both the bride and groom wear their finest clothes. Perhaps the bride wears a traditional costume—layers of white petticoats under a velvet skirt, a hand-embroidered blouse, a brightly colored wool shawl, and black patent-leather shoes. A brown derby hat completes her outfit.

In the American Southwest, a traditional Hopi marriage began very simply. The bride moved into the groom's household and ground cornmeal for his family, while his male relatives wove her marriage clothes. When the weaving was finished, she and her husband would go to live permanently with her family. To punish the bride for stealing their nephew, the groom's aunts attacked his house with water and mud in a mock battle. How could their nephew marry such a lazy girl! they asked. Why were his mother and sisters allowing her to take him away?

After four days the mothers of the bride and groom washed the couple's hair together in one basin, with soap made from the yucca plant. While their hair was mingled together to symbolize their union, the mud-slinging aunts attacked again. All in fun, they tried to separate the couple or to stick their own heads in the basin. When the fun was over and their hair was dry, the couple went to the edge of the Hopi mesa and prayed to the sun. On their return the wife made corn bread for her mother-in-law. Although there were further rites on days to come and more exchanges of gifts between the families, the couple were now husband and wife.

Getting married is a step that may call for a solemn religious rite or involve nothing more than an arrangement between two families. Married life may begin with gala festivities involving thousands of people or with simple ceremonies performed by kinfolk. In any case, it is certain that the bride and groom will always remember the occasion that promised them companionship, security, and a home for future children.

CHAPTER 6

Members of the Wedding

The stars of the wedding ceremony are the bride and groom, but their kinfolk play important roles before and after the marriage. Sometimes parents make all the important marriage decisions. They choose their child's mate, and they expect the newlyweds to live with them.

Sometimes the parents' only job is to give advice about a marriage proposal or to pay for the wedding. Other family members—brothers and sisters, aunts and uncles—play large or small roles in a couple's married life, depending on the society in which they live.

In some places a man may have several wives, and a bride must adjust to a household of co-wives who form a community of their own. More rarely, in some places a

woman lives with more than one husband—usually brothers.

In most industrialized countries of the West, a couple's marriage has little impact on their extended family. Most young people don't depend on a network of relatives for jobs and housing. They expect to find their own mates at work or at school, and to marry for love and companionship. Newlyweds want to live independently in a home of their own. A girl's father may be asked for her hand, and he may give her away at the altar, but these acts are merely polite conventions. Brothers and sisters might be ushers or bridesmaids in the wedding party, but, like their parents, they have no veto power over the match itself.

In China and Japan, on the other hand, a close-knit extended family has always been the ideal. Traditionally, marriages were arranged by parents, and the bride came to live with the groom's family. Her first act in her new home was to kneel at a shrine con-

A Bedouin man, seated at right, with his two wives and children.

taining wooden tablets inscribed with the names of her husband's family ancestors. From the time she married, a woman stopped worshipping her own ancestral spirits and venerated those of her husband.

A Chinese or Japanese bride was put to work in the household under her mother-in-law's supervision. An unlucky girl might be treated as little more than an unpaid servant. In Japan it was said that a daughter-in-law should not be given charge of the housework until she could make miso soup by the family's rules. And before the 1900s in China and Japan, a bride might even be sent back to her parents if her in-laws thought that their son was too devoted to her and neglected them.

Strong family ties remain important in China and Japan. In the 1990s about half of Chinese newlyweds lived with parents, most often the groom's. Young working couples depend on parents for help with housework and for child care. Sons are still expected to support their parents and grandparents if necessary. Partly for this reason and partly because of the tradition of ancestor worship, parents-to-be hope that their child will be a son.

In India it remains customary for the bride to join her husband's family household. At the end of her festive wedding, the bride often wails heartbrokenly as she says goodbye to her parents. She is going off to live in a house full of strangers, where she must adjust to a whole new family. If hers is a properly arranged marriage, she knows little about her husband as well. As a new bride she is expected to be demure, obedient, and silent. It is no wonder that her wedding day is a time of mixed emotions.

The same submissive attitude is expected of a bride in the Middle East. She often lives with her in-laws. Her mother-in-law demands respect and unquestioning obedience. A wedding night tradition in one rural Egyptian community demonstrates the power a mother-in-law has over her son's bride. As the girl arrives at her husband's house, his mother stands in the doorway and blocks the entrance with a raised leg. The bride must crawl into her new home.

In Turkey a newlywed girl is called *gelin*, a word that means "Come!" Except for young children, her position is the lowest in the household. In rural areas she does the housework or works in her husband's family fields under her mother-in-law's direction. She is not free to come and go as she pleases. She must ask permission to visit her own parents, even if they live nearby. One bride who was denied such permission made the mistake of arguing with her mother-in-law. As punishment she was not allowed to visit anyone for three months.

A woman may be called gelin for as long as five years after her wedding. It will be a shorter time if another man in the household marries and a newer bride arrives. Or, her husband may release her from the role of gelin. He will give her a gift and tell her that she is no longer a humble bride but a respected wife.

Rather than joining the groom's family, newlyweds sometimes become members of the wife's family. This was the tradition of the Apache Indians of the Southwest. The bride and her family built a new wickiup for the couple near her parents and married sisters. The whole family helped one another and worked together as a group. Couples who lived outside of a family cluster were pitied. Other Apaches would say, "Poor people, they have no relatives they can live with. That must be why they are living alone."

An Apache man is still expected to help his in-laws and treat them with great respect. He should never look directly at his wife's mother, and she should be careful to keep out of sight when he is nearby. Years ago the game animals he killed and the horses he captured on raids were turned over to his wife's parents. If he didn't live up to his responsibilities, his in-laws might take back his wife.

Also in earlier days, a prominent Apache man might have more than one wife. Often his second wife was his wife's younger sister, offered to him by his in-laws to keep him tied to their family. Besides, the Apaches felt that wives who were sisters were likely to get along better than wives who were strangers. Even if co-wives weren't related, they called each other "sister."

This young girl, suitably veiled, is about to be married in Turkey.

Africa remains the only major world region where *polygamy* (the marriage of a man to more than one woman) is widely practiced. Although most men have only one wife, it is often out of necessity, not choice. Multiple wives are a sign of wealth and success.

In many African countries Islamic marriage laws permit a man to have as many as four wives at a time if he is able to support them. Customarily, his house has separate quarters for men and women, with each wife having her own room around a central courtyard. The first, or senior, wife is in charge of running the household. A new wife must bend to her decisions about domestic chores. Co-wives take turns cooking and, if they get along, help each other with housework and child care. Since the activities of men and women are highly segregated, a woman spends more time in the company of the co-wives than she does with her husband. If co-wives quarrel, it is not usually about love or jealousy of their husband's attentions. It is likely to be a squabble over favors for their children or unequal financial treatment.

In northern Nigeria, Muslim women are secluded in the women's quarters of their husband's compound. Nevertheless, many of them earn money by preparing food to sell. Much of the money the women earn is spent on dowry gifts for their daughters.

While in many places a man may have more than one wife, very few societies have permitted *polyandry*, the marriage of a woman to more than one husband. In the past it was a common pattern in central and south Asia. Nowadays, this marriage system is found only among people in the high Himalayas of Nepal. They live in remote farming villages where the growing season is short, rainfall is scarce, and life is hard.

Why do these poor mountain farmers prefer this kind of marriage? One important reason is that a family's land does not have to be divided if all the sons share a wife. Another is that each brother is able to increase the family's income with a different job. One brother may work the family fields, another may take care of their cattle, while still another may be a trader who travels the countryside selling manufactured goods. In this way the whole family enjoys a higher standard of living and gains prestige and political strength.

The wife stays at home, working on the land and taking care of the children. Ideally, she never shows a preference for one of her husbands over another. Her marriage gives her security, care in her old age, and respectability in her community. She hopes it will be said of her that she is "a wise and lucky woman who keeps brothers and sons together."

In Latin America the bride and groom's godparents often play a major role in the wedding. They are expected to contribute important gifts and often to help with the wedding expenses. Godparents are chosen from among the friends or relatives of the family. For the influence and support they can provide, some people ask the most powerful, well-off members of the community to fill this role.

Godparents are especially important to the Maya of Mexico and Central America. In times past the groom's birth godfather might go with his father to negotiate marriage arrangements with the bride's parents. Then, a second set of godparents were chosen as sponsors of the wedding. Both sets of godparents helped pay for the festivities and were interested in the success of the marriage. Newlyweds knew that they would make many people unhappy if their marriage failed.

Like the Maya, some couples in Peru and Bolivia choose a special set of godparents when they marry. These godparents act as advisers and benefactors and help pay for the traditional ceremonies. They may even act as stand-ins for the couple's parents at the civil and religious ceremonies. However, the gift-giving and responsibilities are not a one-way street. A couple owe their godparents deep respect and must work for them whenever they ask.

What's Ahead?

Wedding announcements in newspapers tell the story of how marriage has changed and point to more changes in the future. Not so long ago, the bride's job—if she had one—was never mentioned. Today's papers tell us about brides whose professional positions match the groom's occupation in importance. Often, too, the couple work in the same field. Also, more and more brides and grooms are marrying for a second time (or more). Another trend has been an increase in the number of racial, ethnic, and religious intermarriages. And a still further sign of the changing times is that many of the wedding ceremonies are performed by women ministers, rabbis, or judges.

Why is the way we marry changing? The answer lies in the fact that social changes influence whom we marry, when we marry, and even how many children we have. Once people everywhere looked to their family to satisfy most of their needs. The family worked together as a unit, children's labor was needed, kinfolk lived nearby, and the family took care of its sick or elderly members. Today our homes are no longer our whole world. In most places, responsibilities that were once the family's now belong to organizations such as schools, hospitals, and government welfare agencies.

Perhaps the most obvious change in our society—and in much of the rest of the world as well—is the increasing economic and political power of women. In the past, a woman had to marry if she wanted financial support and children. Her standard of living depended on whether she married a wealthy banker or a poor farmer. She had little control over the number of children she had and was probably pregnant or caring for a small child for most of her short married life. In the 1700s a couple could expect to live together for an average of twelve years before one of them died.

In many parts of the world, today's woman can support herself, and birth control gives her a choice over the size of her family. In the early nineteenth century, an American mother had an average of seven children; by the mid twentieth century the number had dropped to two. In the last half of the twentieth century, there has been a tremendous increase in the number of wives who share the job of family provider. By the 1990s two thirds of American wives had jobs, and the percentage was going up.

With women's financial independence have come higher expectations about married life. More and more women expect to share not only the role of provider but also the chores connected with housework and child care. This new pattern requires both men and women to change their traditional roles. Women can expect to work outside their home for their whole life. Many men are now doing things they've never been expected to do before, such as care for a baby or learn how to cook and clean.

Today both men and women put a high value on a loving, companionable relationship with their spouses. With financial independence possible for both partners, there are fewer reasons for people to stay in unhappy marriages. Consequently, the divorce rate has increased along with people's expectations for an emotionally gratifying marriage. Half of American marriages now end in divorce, and it appears that the divorce rate will remain high in the future.

Quite recently there has been a surge in the number of interracial couples who fall in love and marry. This trend shows how much ideas about race and marriage have changed since 1967 when the United States Supreme Court struck down state laws against interracial marriage. At that time nineteen states still had such laws. In 1960 less than 2 percent of African-Americans were married to whites. In 1990 the number had climbed to almost 6 percent and was rising.

Another new development is the growing number of couples who live together before marriage. Only fifty years ago, it was common to get married right after high school or college. Today young people are marrying later, and living together is sometimes the first step toward marriage.

As the world grows more industrialized and urban, marriage traditions everywhere are changing. In many countries the marriage age continues to increase, and the power of parents to arrange marriages continues to decline. Today the average Japanese bride is nearly twenty-six years old. Only thirty years ago she would have been considered "over the hill" as far as marriage was concerned. India, also, has a rising marriage age as more families look for educated girls as wives for their sons. And in China's cities nine of ten marriages are now free-choice matches. The freedom to chose a spouse is due, in part, to the victory of the government's marriage regulations over old-fashioned traditions. Today young people in China can call on political organizations for help if their parents object to their choice of a spouse.

In Africa more and more people are crowding into cities for jobs. New roads, modern communication, and education have made villages less isolated. As a result, traditional marriage systems are being abandoned. Nowadays, families

There are no racial barriers for this young couple in love.

who still demand bridewealth for a daughter's hand are apt to want cash, not the old-fashioned gifts of cattle or other goods. A groom may be asked for help with his wife's school fees or her parents' taxes or medical bills. Many women try to avoid bridewealth marriages altogether. They are able to earn money on their own and insist on a greater say about their marriage partners. And educated women are less likely to accept a marriage in which they have to share their husband with other wives.

In some parts of Africa, however, newly independent countries brought back old marriage customs that were outlawed by colonial governments. These changes came as a reaction to the lack of respect colonial powers paid to African cultural traditions. Polygamy and bridewealth payments, for example, are once again being practiced in Mozambique.

As the saying goes, the more things change, the more they stay the same. This French couple chose to follow tradition for their wedding ceremony.

There are similar changes in parts of the Middle East. New Islamic governments in Iran and Iraq passed laws that returned control over daughters and wives to fathers and husbands. In 1982 new regulations in Iraq made it illegal for a married women to travel without her husband. Unmarried women had to have the written consent of their fathers or guardians. And women were told it was their patriotic duty to have five children.

In another Islamic country, Saudi Arabia, traditions are changing to allow women more freedom in marriage arrangements. In the past Saudi parents took no steps to marry off their daughters. Unmarried girls were never seen at social gatherings. The respectable thing to do was to wait for a proposal from a boy's parents. Today a girl's mother and father take a more active role in her marriage arrangements. Women take their daughters to weddings and big receptions so other women with eligible sons will see them. And, nowadays, Saudi girls have more say about whom they will marry. A girl's refusal may end marriage negotiations. But it is very unusual for a girl to marry against her parents' wishes. To refuse a match is permissible, but for a daughter to make her own choice is disgraceful.

Older Saudi couples had separate living quarters and separate entertainment. A married woman spent most of her time with female friends. Today couples spend more time together. A wife accompanies her husband on visits to friends.

She has more say about their household budget and their children's education. She might even ignore her mother-in-law's wishes on certain issues!

In our rapidly changing world, what's ahead for marriage? How people marry varies with the changing communities in which they live, so we can't expect them to marry the same way in the future. Nevertheless, certain trends seem to be nearly universal. Looking ahead, we might find that people everywhere marry later, have fewer children, and hope for companionship and, of course, for love.

For Further Reading

Arnold, Caroline. *How People Get Married*, Franklin Watts, 1987

Bennett, Olivia. *Sikh Wedding*, Trafalgar, 1991

Drucker, Malka. *Celebrating Life: Jewish Rites of Passage*, Holiday House, 1984

Emrich, Duncan. *The Folklore of Weddings and Marriage*, American Heritage Press, 1970

Faces: The Magazine About People, Getting Married, Vol. 3, No. 9, June 1987

Larson, Heidi. *Wedding Time*, Trafalgar, 1991

Lasker, Joe. *Marry Every After: The Story of Two Medieval Weddings*, Viking Press, 1976

Morris, Ann. *Weddings*, Lothrop, Lee & Shepard, 1995

Index

About the Author

Carol Gelber is the author of *Masks Tell Stories*, published by The Millbrook Press, and has also written many articles for *Faces*, a children's anthropology magazine. She has worked as a scientific assistant in the anthropology department of the American Museum of Natural History in New York City, and is a volunteer reading tutor in the New York public schools.

While writing *Love and Marriage Around the World*, Carol Gelber's daughter was married in a ceremony that blended new trends with old traditions. The bride wore white but replaced the customary veil with flowers. The officiating minister was a woman, and the "bridesmaids" were male friends. Nevertheless, as this photograph shows, the solemnity of the occasion never changes. The nervous bride is slipping the groom's ring on the wrong finger!